THE CIVIL WAR HISTORY SERIES

ATLANTA
A PORTRAIT OF THE CIVIL WAR

The quarters of the 22nd Massachusetts, Major General William T. Sherman's provost guard, occupy the grounds of Atlanta City Hall in the fall of 1864 following a four-month campaign. The city became a comfortable refuge for Federal forces, offering staff the luxury of residential homes while the troops enjoyed ample huts constructed of their own shelter-half tents combined with lumber, windows, and other materials scavenged from local homes and businesses.

THE CIVIL WAR HISTORY SERIES

ATLANTA
A PORTRAIT OF THE CIVIL WAR

MICHAEL ROSE
ATLANTA HISTORY CENTER

TEMPUS

Copyright © 1999 by the Atlanta Historical Society.
ISBN 0-7385-0138-7

Published by Arcadia Publishing,
an imprint of Tempus Publishing, Inc.
2 Cumberland Street
Charleston, SC 29401

Printed in Great Britain.

Library of Congress Catalog Card Number: 99-61840

For all general information contact Arcadia Publishing at:
Telephone 843-853-2070
Fax 843-853-0044
E-Mail arcadia@charleston.net

For customer service and orders:
Toll-Free 1-888-313-BOOK

Visit us on the internet at http://www.arcadiaimages.com

Atlanta History Center
130 West Paces Ferry Road
Atlanta, Georgia 30305-1366
(404) 814-4000
http://www.atlhist.org

Contents

Introduction   7

1. The City in the Forest   9

2. The War Grows Near   37

3. The City under Siege   63

4. Yankees in Atlanta   91

5. Destruction   115

Acknowledgments and Resources   128

George N. Barnard's portable darkroom appears at right in a view of Confederate works looking east to the site of the Battle of Bald Hill (Atlanta). Soldiers, possibly from the XX Corps, sit around reading, playing cards, drinking, and napping in the sun. The XX Corps were the first troops to enter the city. Transferring from the Virginia front, the corps suffered from a history of defeat. The success of the Atlanta campaign, therefore, brought them their first taste of victory. "At 11 A.M." wrote Samuel Bechtel of the XX, they ". . . marched into the once beleaguered 'Gate-City of the South' & claimed it as their prize."

Many of this book's views of Atlanta's defenses were taken by George N. Barnard or his staff during the Federal occupation of Atlanta, September–November 1864, and again in 1866 as he planned a publication of war views. Except when noted, the portrait photographers are unknown, as is the case with most Southern portraits of the period. Because Atlanta has a long history of altering street names, original names are given with their current designations in brackets.

INTRODUCTION
Images and Icons

Atlanta is unique in Civil War history. Whereas most Civil War battles were fought in country fields and woods, the battles for Atlanta were fought in what was then, like now, an urban area. Unlike the rural battlefields commemorated today with parks, monuments, and reenactments, 130 years of development and urban sprawl have largely overtaken old city streets, period homes, and military fortifications. In Atlanta, only the pictures remain.

When the public envisions Atlanta during the Civil War, two primary images—of two unparalleled individuals—dominate: William Tecumseh Sherman and Scarlett O'Hara. The visual imagery of both characters is powerful. The scowling, haggard features of Sherman, the "war is Hell" commander who leveled the city and is hated by some to this day, is an effective icon for the depiction of the Atlanta campaign. Perhaps only representations of Robert E. Lee (*the* Southern icon) and Ulysses S. Grant come close to achieving Sherman's symbolic significance.

Scarlett O'Hara is something else altogether. The pervading presence of *Gone with the Wind* is everywhere in the mass culture concept of Civil War Atlanta. The motion picture version of the novel supplied a concrete visual element: graceful Southern mansions, war-weary Scarlett racing along Peachtree Street, and Rhett battling the fires of Sherman's destruction. *Gone with the Wind* created a legendary image of Atlanta—one readers and movie viewers believe in only too well.

This popular perception of 1860s Atlanta is incomplete. There is more to the city's Civil War heritage than a frowning general and a wily gentlewoman. *Atlanta: A Portrait of the Civil War* completes the story, presenting images of the city as it was up to and during the Civil War. These are views of Atlanta placed within the context of the war experience and portraits of Atlanta's residents that reinforce the human component of the conflict. The book includes images familiar to Civil War enthusiasts as well: the ruins of the Ponder House, the destruction of the rail lines, and the demolition of General Hood's ordnance train—all frequently used to illustrate the Civil War as a whole. Taken together, these images create a picture of Civil War Atlanta.

Martha Lumpkin was the youngest daughter of Georgia Governor Wilson Lumpkin (served 1831–35). In December 1843, the settlement of Terminus was officially named Marthasville in her honor. But residents soon considered the name too provincial for their growing city, and officials of the Western & Atlantic Railroad began calling their local depot "Atlanta." By coincidence, Martha's middle name was "Atalanta," the powerful huntress of Greek legend, so many residents still believed the town to be named for her.

One
THE CITY IN THE FOREST

Atlanta was, and still is, a transportation town. In 1837, long before the city was the arsenal of the Civil War, a cotton capital, or the harbinger of the New South, it was a small community in the southern wilderness. Terminus, the nickname applied to the original settlement, described its location at the literal end of the rail line—a yet-to-be-built railroad running north through the Georgia Piedmont. But with the arrival of the first railroad in 1845 came a change in the town, from terminal to junction—stimulating commerce, capital, and immigration in the region.

In 1843, upon the receipt of a U.S. post office and the community's incorporation, the town once known as Terminus obtained the hopelessly rustic and decidedly un-picturesque designation of Marthasville. It was almost too much for the locals to stand. By late 1845, the Western & Atlantic Railroad began using the made-up moniker, "Atlanta" (the so-called feminine derivation of the word "Atlantic") on its station sign board—and the title stuck.

Despite growth and diversification, Atlanta remained defined by the railroads. By the close of the 1850s, there were four major lines serving the city and linking the Southeast—the Western & Atlantic, the Georgia Railroad, the Macon & Western, and the Atlanta & West Point. The passenger depot, considered the largest and finest in the South, sat in the very heart of the city, actually straddling the community's public space. (During the Civil War, all Confederate troops from the region would pass through this depot on their way to the front.) The volume of comings and goings through the depot led Atlanta to be known as the "Gate City of the South" by 1857. By 1860, the population boomed to nearly 12,000, and Atlanta's commercial base boasted industrial rolling mills, cotton gins, sawmills, tanneries, banks, insurance agencies, engineers, and the usual allotment of attorneys.

But the boom would not last. On January 2, 1861, more than 60 percent of Atlantans elected a pro-secession delegation to the state convention to decide the question of national unity. The representatives, including former Atlanta Mayor Luther J. Glenn, gathered in Milledgeville, Georgia, in mid-January and overwhelmingly adopted the ordinance of secession. Atlanta's experience in the Civil War was about to begin. (Ironically, the pro-Union delegates in the election were led by Atlanta's destined Civil War mayor, James M. Calhoun.)

This is the left side of a three-part panorama taken from the dome of the Atlanta Female Institute. The cupola-topped building at upper left is the Atlanta Medical College (p. 126), and the two-story building at center is the Calico House (p. 25). Built in 1860, the female seminary

became a hospital in 1863 and was demolished by the Federal army for its bricks, which were used to construct chimneys for the army's winter quarters (p. 2).

Shown here is the panorama looking to the city center. The city's commercial district is located toward the photo's upper left horizon; barely visible is the Car Shed passenger depot (p. 27). The residence at lower right belongs to architect John Boutell Jr. (p. 30). The unpaved street

running across the bottom of the photograph is Collins [Courtland] Street. Most Atlanta streets remained unpaved until 1882.

In the final part of the panorama, the street running into the distance is Ellis, crossing Ivy Street [Peachtree Center Avenue] in the middle and cresting at the ridge, marking Peachtree Street. Note the open ground providing space for gardening and livestock. At the corner of Ellis and

Peachtree is the residence of Dr. Chapmon Powell (p. 28); the columned house next to it is the Austin Leyden home (p. 112–3)—long since demolished, it is the current site of Macy's downtown department store.

Descended from Franco-German stock, in 1848 watchmaker Er Lawshé (right) moved to Atlanta, where he opened a jewelry store on Whitehall Street. Lawshé and his family, including wife Sarah Winifred Peck (opposite) and son William Peck Lawshé (below), lived on Peachtree near Cain Street. Commissioned a captain in Company E, 3rd Battalion of the Georgia State Guards, Lawshé sent his family to Augusta for the war's duration. Shortly after the war, the Lawshé residence was requisitioned as headquarters for the commander of the Post of Atlanta, Prince Felix Salm-Salm, a Federal brigadier general from Prussia.

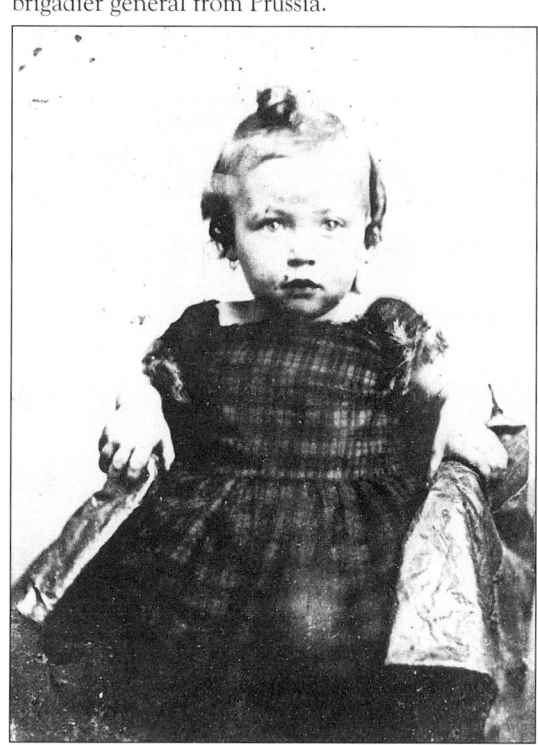

An Atlanta fire company poses on city property at the corner of Alabama and Pryor Streets, c. 1853. Commonly known as Humbug Square, the lot was a popular center for public speakers, circuses, medicine shows, and auctions. The area to the right is the city's State Square, and the frame building at center is the first train depot. Atlanta's first volunteer fire company organized in 1850 in order to replace bucket brigades with its fire engine, "Blue Dick." A few years later, it built a fire station at Market [South Broad] Street and the rail line near the current Five Points MARTA station.

Looking up muddy Decatur Street, the Trout House and pedimented Masonic Hall stand at right. In 1859, Edward E. Rawson (p. 103), owner of a two-story building across from city park, offered the Masons a meeting place if they added a third floor at their expense. During the war, the building was saved through the efforts of local members appealing to fraternal comrades in the Federal army.

Principal assistant to Georgia Railroad Chief Engineer J. E. Thomson and later the railroad's superintendent, Richard Peters (left) helped develop the city into a transportation center. Moving to Atlanta in 1846, he purchased a residence (above) at Mitchell and Forsyth Streets. In the 1850s, Peters acquired property that included the current sites of the Fox Theatre, the Coca-Cola Company, and Georgia Tech. Thomson, Peters's employer, is the man credited for coining the name "Atlanta."

This view was taken looking south on Whitehall Street in Atlanta's central business district. A lamppost at the corner of Alabama Street signifies the city's progress; Atlanta obtained gas lighting in 1856 with the incorporation of the Atlanta Gas Light Company.

Atlanta residents were proud of their dignified—if reserved—city hall, remarking it reflected "great credit on the city authority." Erected by Columbus Hughes in 1854, the building also served as the Fulton County Court House in rather cramped quarters. After surviving the war, the building was demolished in 1884 to make way for the current state capitol.

Here, Piromis Hulsey Bell, son of Mary Jane Hulsey Bell and Marcus Aurelius Bell (opposite), perches precariously on a stand and grasps a chair. This sixth-plate ambrotype accompanies a locket of Bell's hair and a swatch of fabric from his clothing.

In 1860, attorney and realtor Marcus Bell built the Calico House at Wheat and Collins Streets [Auburn Avenue and Courtland Street]. Surmounted by a cupola, the residence was constructed of plaster-covered stone and marbleized in shades of blue, yellow, and red. Atlantans, however, believed the effect looked more like calico fabric than classic marble, hence the home's nickname. During the war, Bell contracted typhoid while serving as adjutant to General Howell Cobb in Collier's Guards of the Georgia Infantry.

Mary Jane Hulsey Bell is shown with an infant Piromis, named for an Egyptian term signifying an honest and virtuous man, according to ancient Greek historian Herodotus. Marcus Bell's own brothers included Jedediah Flavius, Lycurus Mucklesworth, and Margenius Assyrumus.

In 1842, contractor Thomas George Washington Cruselle built the first house on Decatur Street. A native of Washington, D.C., he erected the original Western & Atlantic Railroad bridge across the Chattahoochee River, as well as the Macon & Western Railroad station, the state railroad shops, and the Calico House. In 1864, Cruselle assisted Mayor Calhoun when he surrendered the city.

Julia Anne Rice, married in 1858, was the second wife of Thomas Cruselle. Her brother, Frank P. Rice, a bookbinder by trade, was responsible for the painted marbleized effect of the Calico House.

A *Harper's Weekly* scene of the railroad yard in Atlanta depicts Cruselle's Macon & Western Railroad station at right center. The station was known as the Rock Depot to distinguish it from the brick construction of the Car Shed, at left, across the rail lines.

During the war, the Calico House was a center of activity, providing both work space and storage for clothing, food, ammunition, and medical supplies; a wing attached to the rear of the house served as a hospital. During the Federal occupation, it also served as the headquarters for Orlando M. Poe, Sherman's chief engineer.

In the early 1850s, cotton dealer Alexander Weldon Mitchell played an important part in the victory of the "Moral" party over the "Free and Rowdy" faction in city politics. Their success resulted in relocation of Atlanta's "rough" segment from Murrell's Row—located along Decatur Street west of Pryor—to the infamous Snake Nation in the Castleberry Hill district of Atlanta.

With the development of the city's rail network, its importance as an agricultural market grew. Settling at Terminus in 1843, William Gadsen Forsyth (right) and his brother, Ambrose, were the city's first cotton merchants. William Forsyth was called into service with Company A of the 2nd Georgia Reserves during the last year of the war. Forsyth Street in downtown Atlanta is named for Ambrose.

The Car Shed, built by the Western & Atlantic Railroad, is seen from the first bridge to be built over the tracks. The wooden bridge spanned the downtown rail lines between Bridge Street north of the tracks to Market Street running south. The path across the upper center of the image is the crossing from Peachtree to Whitehall Street. Since all other rail crossings were at street grade, getting from one side of town to the other could be either quite slow or quite dangerous. Designed by Edward A. Vincent and completed in 1854, the depot was large enough to include the tracks of all four rail lines serving Atlanta.

After moving to Atlanta in 1850, Dr. Chapmon Powell built a residence at the corner of Peachtree and Ellis Streets, which he shared with his daughter, Martha Ann Jincie Powell. Martha lived to age 87 and was known throughout the region for her decorative needlework.

In 1856, Martha Powell married Dr. Fielding Travis Powell, a distant relative, who served as a surgeon with the Confederate army. This daguerreotype was made by George A. Jeffers, a northern photographer who migrated south, settling in Savannah in 1859.

Architect John Boutell Jr. moved to the city in 1852, building a house on Collins [Courtland] at Ellis Street. With an extensive lot running behind, the house site provided space for rare flowers and shrubbery he brought from his commissions in Charleston, Macon, and Savannah.

Boutell built a number of important structures, including the city barracks, Atlanta Medical College (p. 126), and houses for John Neal (p. 110), Ephraim Ponder (p. 84–5), and Austin Leyden (p. 112–3). During the war, he assisted in the construction of the city defenses while his wife and daughters volunteered in the hospitals, including the Calico House, just a few blocks south of their home.

Shown here affectionately holding hands, printer Thomas Stephens Reynolds and his wife, Mary King, lived at McDonough Street [Capitol Avenue] and Clark Alley, an area now lost in the freeways south of downtown. A native of Lexington, Georgia, Reynolds worked as foreman of the *Athens* [Ga.] *Banner* and in the 1840s established a newspaper in Macon, after which he obtained the lucrative trade of printing the Georgia state court reports. After developing a power press, Reynolds relocated to Atlanta where he invented an envelope printer and founded a short-lived newspaper, the *Atlanta Independent*.

In front of his house at Collins and Wheat Streets [Courtland and Auburn Avenue], William P. Orme sits in his carriage next to Henry Allan Rucker, born a slave in Athens, Georgia. After the war, Rucker attended Atlanta University and was a delegate to the Republican party convention of 1880. During much of the 1880s, Rucker clerked in the internal revenue office in Atlanta, and served as collector of internal revenue for the District of Georgia from 1896 to 1910.

Orme was secretary and treasurer of the Atlanta & West Point Railroad. The West Point rail line became the target of Sherman's flanking maneuvers in late July 1864, resulting in the Battle of Ezra Church. Moving farther south, Federal troops struck the line at Fairburn and put the railroad out of commission.

The brother of William P. Orme, Dr. Francis Hodgson Orme (below), a homeopathic physician, moved to Atlanta in 1861, where he lived with his wife, Ellen Woodward (right), at Forsyth and Luckie Streets, the current site of the Rialto Theater. During the war, Orme served as 2nd lieutenant in Alexander's Cavalry, a local defense unit. Years later, he acted as Henry W. Grady's physician, attending to the famed journalist at the time of his death.

Dr. Benjamin F. Bomar was elected Atlanta's second mayor in 1849 and later served as clerk of the Fulton County Superior Court. Bomar and his wife, Sarah Elizabeth Lumpkin Haynes (opposite), lived along Marietta Road, one mile from the city line. During the siege of Atlanta, their home was located close to the military lines, placing them among the thickest of the shelling. His daguerreotype frame is stamped by Barnes; it was possibly made by Chauncey Barnes, who worked in Mobile, Alabama, in the 1850s.

Like many Southern wives and sweethearts, Laura Thompson Chapman sent her beloved off to war with a keepsake as an expression of love and support. Laura made a Bible marker for her husband, George Reed Chapman, which read "I Love Thee." Chapman carried it with him until severely wounded at the Battle of the Wilderness in May 1864.

Two
THE WAR GROWS NEAR

In May 1862, Atlanta became a post of the Military Division of Georgia. To guard government supplies and preserve order, regulations called for city guard details, railroad sentinels, and prohibitions against providing liquor to officers and soldiers. By late summer, General Braxton Bragg declared martial law. On September 3, the inspector general's office in Richmond suspended the writ of habeas corpus in Atlanta "and for five miles around its corporate limits." War, if not the actual fighting, had arrived in Atlanta.

The city by this time had become a medical and convalescent center for the South, with as many as 26 hospitals. Atlanta also served as the Confederacy's workplace for manufacturing, offering mills, plants, and factories turning out everything from buttons and canteens to railroad cars and ironclad plating. While city residents had begun to flee to safer locales, Atlanta's population, fed by transient, war-time inhabitants, steadily increased to more than 20,000.

Amidst this activity of war, Atlanta women organized the Ladies' Soldiers' Relief Society and the Atlanta Hospital Association to administer to the dying, nurse the sick, and support the troops. The women provided soup, coffee, and milk to hungry soldiers and the trainloads of wounded. The women also produced clothing for the soldiers and performed needed tasks, such as sewing, rolling bandages, knitting socks, and sending food, medicine, and—surprisingly—wine and other spirits to the front line.

Yet even with war, Atlanta resident Eugenia Goode noted, "all was not gloom and tears." Atlantans found time for picnics at Vinings Station, Stone Mountain, and Walton Springs, where bands played *Lorena*, *Beautiful Dreamer*, and *Rest, Darling, Rest*.

However, in April 1863 came the war's first push into Georgia. A Federal raid led by Colonel Abel Streight attempted to cut the Western & Atlantic rail line south of Dalton, only 80 miles from Atlanta. While the raid failed, it caused considerable alarm in Atlanta. With the fall of Vicksburg in July, Confederate authorities, foreseeing the transfer of Federal troops from the Mississippi theater, pursued the fortification of Atlanta. Under the supervision of Lemuel P. Grant and Moses H. Wright, the army constructed a defensive line surrounding the city.

War came to Georgia at the Battle of Chickamauga in late 1863. Though Chickamauga was a Southern victory, the Federal army won battles at Lookout Mountain and Missionary Ridge in November and broke free of Chattanooga, 120 miles from Atlanta. Many considered the mountainous terrain too difficult for the Yankees to easily pass through. "The country from Chattanooga to this place is very rough and covered with woods," wrote Sergeant William Jack of Connecticut, "right in front of us is a ridge of mountains and a few miles on the other side are the Rebs . . . ."

Attorney Luther J. Glenn (opposite) was elected mayor of Atlanta in 1858, serving two terms. Glenn practiced law in Henry County and served in the state legislature before moving to Atlanta in 1851. Following Sherman's departure from Atlanta in December 1864, a detachment of Southern troops, including Company C of Cobb's Legion, occupied the city with Glenn as post commander. On May 4, 1865, he surrendered the last remaining troops, permanently ending Confederate control of the city. Glenn's son Judson (above) is shown in his Confederate-style uniform.

Levi Cohen (opposite), a native of Germany, immigrated to America in 1850 and settled in Dalton, Georgia, working as a tinsmith and making canteens at the beginning of the war. In 1862 he moved to Atlanta and established a dry goods business. After the war, Cohen was instrumental in founding the Hebrew Benevolent Congregation, holding the first organizational meeting in his home. For nearly eight years he served as the president of the Jewish congregation, commonly known as The Temple.

Sarah Soloman Cohen (above), the wife of Levi Cohen, was a native of Savannah and was president of the Hebrew Sabbath School; Hennie Cohen (left) was their adopted daughter.

One of the city's first physicians, Dr. Joshua Gilbert moved to Marthasville in 1845, opening an office on Marietta Street. When traveling on horseback, he blew a whistle to alert prospective patients of his passing. Gilbert served on the first board of health, and, as a member of the Civil War committee of safety, he donated time to care for families of servicemen.

A Virginia native, Dr. Thomas Spencer Powell was instrumental in the establishment of the Atlanta Medical College, where he later served as professor of obstetrics. Like Dr. Gilbert (above), he offered services to families of Confederate volunteers. As the city became a medical center, all Atlanta doctors found themselves treating soldiers and providing for residents during the siege.

William and Sarah Solomon lived in an impressive house on the corner of Crew [Capitol Place] and Mitchell Streets, opposite city hall. Solomon, from Zebulon, Georgia, was a private banker and realtor with a local reputation as a successful gambler as well. William Solomon died in 1874 following a fall from a second-story window at his home, reportedly while trying to close the sash. In July 1865, Mrs. Solomon kept busy baking cakes for a "Yankee party" given by Princess Agnes Leclerq Salm-Salm, wife of the Prussian noble who was then Federal commander in Atlanta.

In August 1863, Colonel Lemuel P. Grant (above), chief engineer of the military department of Georgia, and Colonel Moses H. Wright, commander of the Atlanta garrison, undertook construction of defensive fortifications designed to encircle the city. The scene on the opposite page overlooks a landscape filled with trenches and other works, leading Sherman's own chief engineer, Orlando M. Poe, to observe the entrenchments were "too strong to assault and too extensive to invest." Colonel Grant developed a perimeter defense line consisting of 17 redoubts (designated A–R) connected by a sequence of rifle trenches. Eventually, Grant completed more than 10 miles of defense works averaging 1 mile from the city center. In a memo to him, Colonel Wright (p. 61) notified Grant such defenses would require more than 55,000 troops just to man the line.

Following through this chapter is a series of photographs taken by George N. Barnard displaying the Confederate defenses after they fell to Federal forces. The following military terms are used in the identification of the fortifications: *abatis*, felled trees with branches pointed toward the enemy; *chevaux-de-frise*, spiked logs; and *fraises*, slanted stakes.

The camp of the 1st Michigan Engineers sits beyond Fort Walker, a large salient located in present-day Grant Park. Named for Major General William H. T. Walker, killed in the Battle of Bald Hill (Atlanta), this is one of the few remnants of the Confederate defensive line.

With one man on duty, troops relax in a Confederate fort overlooking the Western & Atlantic Railroad, running northwest out of Atlanta. This was the city's original rail line, terminating at Chattanooga.

Here, two men sit on head logs near Confederate rifle trenches protecting the Georgia Railroad. The railway sits in a deep, steep-sided cut just beyond the trench at left; at left center can be seen just the smokestack of a locomotive. Head logs allowed troops to fire under them while protecting their heads from enemy fire. The skid poles lying across the pit offered safety in case the logs were dislodged.

A locomotive sits stranded along the Georgia Railroad east of the city, its rail line destroyed ahead and behind. Viewed from a Confederate parapet near Decatur, the approach to the entrenchment is protected by a row of *abatis*.

An avid secessionist and states' rights advocate, Alexander McGhee Wallace (opposite) was captain of the Atlanta Greys. He resigned in January 1861 to accept a commission as captain of Company L, 1st Georgia Regiment. At the time of Confederate President Jefferson Davis's visit to Atlanta in 1861, Wallace served as an organizer and host of the welcoming committee. Wounded at the Battle of Missionary Ridge, November 1863, he was invalided and returned to Atlanta. During the war, Wallace maintained a regular correspondence with his wife, Frances Singleton (above). Referring to her as "my precious wife" and other terms of affection, he once closed by stating, "I miss the presence of my children at night and in all the bustle of the day, Your dear face and all the precious memories connected with it are ever present with me."

Here, two soldiers stand atop Confederate Fort H guarding Marietta Street and the Western & Atlantic rail line running northwest of the city. The approach to the fort is protected by a series of *fraises*, *chevaux-de-frise*, *abatis*, and at left foreground, a white picket fence.

Shown here is a view from inside Confederate Fort H looking down at the Marietta road. In this scene, the embrasure in the breastwork, normally open for artillery placement, has been secured with sandbags as protection against heavy Federal fire.

Another ground-level view of Confederate Fort H clearly displays the *chevaux-de-frise* placed as a barricade across Marietta Street. Photographer George Barnard's portable darkroom can be seen at the center of the photograph, along with his wagon at left.

As well as Fort H, Confederate Fort G, located north of the present-day Georgia World Congress Center, protected the Western & Atlantic Railroad, which crosses diagonally in the foreground.

A descendant of early settlers, Dr. Elijah Lewis Connally (opposite page) was the eldest of 16 children of Thomas and Temperence Peacock Connally (left). At the opening of the war, he was a surgeon in Lee's Volunteers and later served as chairman of a medical conscript board.

Following the war, Connally built the Connally Building at Whitehall and Alabama Streets, and was chairman of Atlanta's board of health. In 1874, he married Mary Virginia Brown (left), daughter of Georgia Civil War Governor Joseph E. Brown.

Originally from Athens, Georgia, Columbus W. Motes (opposite) became one of Atlanta's premier photographers following the Civil War, frequently recording many war heroes and other veterans. Serving as 1st lieutenant in Carlton's Company, Troup County Artillery, he carried with him this ninth-plate ambrotype of his future wife, Emily White, with a note stating: "If I unfortunately fall in battle, some one of my associate officers will confer a favor by forwarding this picture to my sister . . . ."

Two dissimilar views of the same Confederate fort are shown here. In one (top), troops relax around the guns and in their tent, possibly in anticipation of another picture (bottom), posing them at gunner's post, indicating the non-threatened situation in which Barnard executed his photographs.

In an unusual scene, a lone sentry sits out in the open watching over Confederate Fort K. The northernmost fort in the line, Fort K straddled Peachtree Street near the present site of the Fox Theatre. Beyond the sentry stretches the long palisade and row of *fraises*, seen on page 44.

A stack of British-made "Enfield" rifles with canteen and haversack top a Confederate redoubt in the vicinity of what is now the Georgia Tech campus. Part of a new Siege Line added in July, the post overlooks a landscape filled with trenches and other defense works.

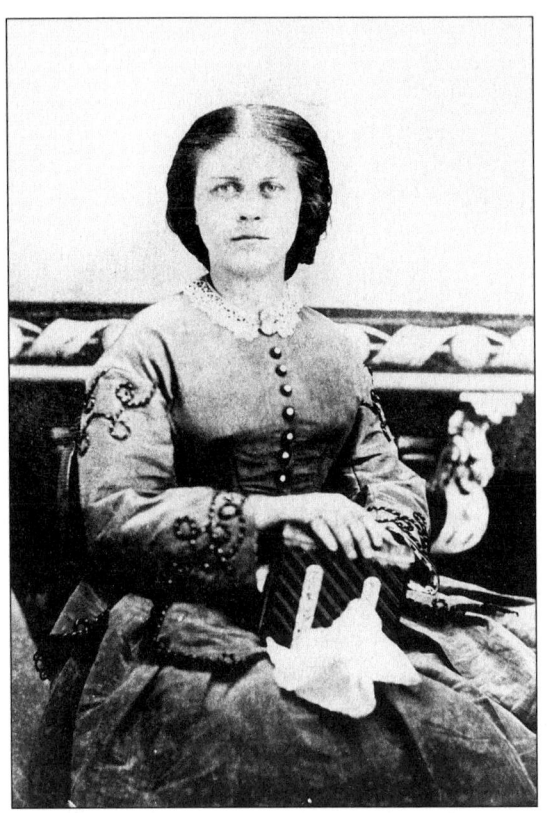

Mayor Calhoun's daughter, Hannah Rebecca Calhoun, married Colonel John H. Mathews of Company B, 28th Georgia Regiment, Army of Tennessee. Mathews's construction company built many postwar buildings, including the home of the *Atlanta Constitution*, the Atlanta Chamber of Commerce, and the Kaiser Building.

During the war, Julia Clayton was one of the social belles of Atlanta. After the war, she helped found the city's Confederate memorial association and was instrumental in arranging the removal of Confederate dead to Oakland Cemetery. In 1866, she married Colonel Edward Foster Hoge of the Lafayette Volunteers, 9th Georgia Regiment, who had been wounded at Gettysburg. In 1883, he established the *Atlanta Journal*; his death shortly afterwards was attributed to his war wounds.

At the beginning of the war, most young Atlanta women continued their lifestyle, attending school and taking part in amateur concerts, parties, the annual May Festival, tableaux, and "gaieties of all kinds." As the war progressed, however, Atlanta's women became well-acquainted with the realities of war, nursing wounded and dying soldiers and facing need and starvation. "We drank sweet potato and chickory coffee," Delia Nichols Foreacre recalled, "and were good at finding substitutes for our favorite beverage of Java and Mocha . . . ."

With the city in the distance, a Federal 12-pound "Napoleon" points out from a Confederate fortification southeast of Atlanta. The wide angle of the embrasure allowed the cannon a broad perspective from which to turn and fire on the enemy. Writing at the end of July, Federal soldier John Dunlap stated his views on the planned offensive: "Well we are in sight of Atlanta but Johnies [sic] hold that place yet—they have strong fortifications but I don't think that we will have to fight them in their works. Our object is to flank them till they will have to come out & fight us . . . ."

Commanding officer of the Atlanta Arsenal, Colonel Moses Hannibal Wright was in charge of the troops and defenses of Atlanta. Graduated seventh in his class at West Point in 1859, he joined the Confederate Ordnance Bureau at the beginning of the war and transferred to Nashville. As commander of the Atlanta Arsenal, Wright was instrumental in developing the city's ability to supply the Confederate war effort. Employing more than 450 people, the arsenal produced over 4 million rounds of ammunition per year and almost 25 million percussion caps. Unfortunately, such success turned the city into the munitions production machine targeted by the Federal army.

In addition to seizing Atlanta, Major General William T. Sherman sought to prevent the transfer of Confederate troops to relieve Robert E. Lee in the struggle against Grant in Virginia. Nevertheless, destruction of the Southern war capability remained a critical element in Grant's war strategy, asserting Sherman's mission was to inflict "all the damage you can against their War resources." Thus this single object within these two goals was Atlanta. Separating Sherman and the city were the north Georgia mountains and the Confederate army.

Three

The City under Siege

After wintering in Tennessee, Sherman moved south in early May 1864. Waiting within fortifications at Dalton was Joseph E. Johnston, head of the Confederate forces. By May 11, he realized Sherman had outflanked him. Confronted with having his lifeline severed behind him —the very rail lines from Atlanta it was his duty to defend—Johnston withdrew deeper into Georgia. This set a pattern for what followed: faced with entrenchments, Sherman maneuvered around Johnston and forced the Confederates closer to Atlanta through Resaca, Adairsville, Cassville, Allatoona Pass, Dallas-New Hope, and Kennesaw Mountain. In two months, he was on the banks of the Chattahoochee River.

In late May, Atlantans were leaving on every outbound train, and men who could not go sent their families to safer places. Sensing the gravity of the situation, Mayor Calhoun called upon all capable men to report for duty. "All male citizens who are not willing to defend their homes and families," he continued, "are requested to leave the city at their earliest convenience . . . ."

By July, the city anticipated Sherman's arrival: "it has been quite evident for some days past," wrote S. P. Richards in his diary, "that there is a great probability of Atlanta falling into the hands of the enemy." On July 8, Federal troops crossed the Chattahoochee forcing Johnston behind Peachtree Creek just outside the city defenses. Within the week, the Federal army destroyed the Georgia Railroad line east of Atlanta. On July 17, Jefferson Davis relieved Johnston of his command for failing "to arrest the advance of the enemy." His replacement, General John B. Hood, attacked Sherman on July 20 at the Battle of Peachtree Creek, and on July 22 at the Battle of Bald Hill (Atlanta). In each engagement, Hood failed to defeat Sherman, who in turn could not break the Confederate hold on the city. Hood abandoned the offensive and withdrew into the city's fortifications.

On July 20, the first shells fell into Atlanta: "We have had a considerable taste of the beauties of bombardment today," noted S. P. Richards a few days later. Stalled on the west side of Atlanta at the Battle of Ezra Church, Sherman's siege intensified; until August 25, the attack continued day and night. From batteries placed on high ground at present-day Eighth Street and Howell Mill Road and Ashby and Simpson Streets, Sherman's artillery bombarded the city.

On August 26, after nearly 40 days of futile operations, Sherman withdrew from his siege lines north and west of Atlanta. With a wide flanking maneuver, he moved against the Macon & Western and Atlanta & West Point, the two remaining rail lines southwest of the city. At Jonesboro, on September 1, Hood's forces were overwhelmed and the last line to Atlanta was cut. By late afternoon, the Confederate withdrawal was under way. Wrote Mary Rawson, "This day witnesses the downfall of the hopes of the citizens of Atlanta."

Lieutenant Hamilton M. Branch of Savannah, 54th Georgia Infantry, was situated in the fortifications along the Chattahoochee River in early July. Writing home, he admitted his lack of knowledge concerning a possible Confederate retreat across the river, but he expressed his confidence in General Johnston: "Old Joe knows what he is at and will take care of us and do what is best."

Confederate fortifications overlook the Chattahoochee River and the Western and Atlantic Railroad bridge originally built by Thomas Cruselle (p. 24). It was here, near where Peachtree Creek flows into the river, that the Native American settlement of Standing Peachtree was situated and from which Peachtree Street derived its name.

This fort, located near Moore's Mill beyond the city, stood in the early defensive line south of the Chattahoochee River. On July 19, Confederate forces evacuated a high bluff south of Moore's Mill, enabling the Federal army to cross Peachtree Creek.

Tanyard Branch, looking downstream toward the site of the original Collier's Mill, was the center of the Battle of Peachtree Creek. Planned by Johnston to be fought in the open ground north of here, the outcome was instead determined in the heavy woods and deep ravines of the Tanyard Branch area.

The crudely marked graves of Federal dead are shown on the battlefield of Peachtree Creek, near present-day Collier Road. Hood's changes to Johnston's original battle plan and poor combat coordination resulted in the first of his failed efforts to stop Sherman.

General Joseph E. Johnston had the unenviable duty to stop Sherman's advance toward Atlanta. Consistently outnumbered, outgunned, and outmaneuvered, Johnston was unable to deliver the counterblow he hoped, and repeatedly retreated south into Georgia. Despite mounting pressure from Confederate President Jefferson Davis to attack Sherman, Johnston sought to preserve his army against the possibility of a devastating defeat by a superior army. Throughout the summer months of 1864, Atlanta residents waited helplessly as the Federal army moved closer to the city.

General John B. Hood, a popular Southern hero, was celebrated for his courageous soldiering at battles such as Gaines's Mill, Gettysburg, and Chickamauga. The same bravery, however, often resulted in presumptuous daring and bold aggressiveness once he became a commander; the recklessness that resulted in his early military success ultimately led to his failure at the battles for Atlanta.

Breastworks outline what is possibly the crest of Bald Hill, where heavy fighting occurred at what is commonly known as the Battle of Atlanta. Hood's attack against Federal troops east of Atlanta was repulsed with disastrous results: the loss of nearly 9,000 men.

Beginning with Chickamauga and Chattanooga, First Lieutenant John A. Bankston fought throughout the Atlanta campaign in Steven's Brigade, Army of Tennessee, until his death July 22 in the Battle of Bald Hill (Atlanta) a few miles from his home. Bankston's family lived north of the stream near the site of the Battle of Utoy Creek, which took place on August 6, 1864.

A DeKalb County native, Brigadier General Charles D. Anderson served with the Beauregard Volunteers in Virginia. Captured at Sharpsburg in 1862, he was exchanged only to be severely wounded at Chancellorsville in 1863. He resigned his commission in early 1864 and was placed in charge of the 3rd Brigade, Georgia Militia, during the siege of Atlanta.

A one-time grocer, Lovick Pierce Thomas Jr. served as lieutenant colonel of the Gwinnett Beauregards, Company A, 42nd Georgia Regiment, until his surrender at Greensboro, North Carolina, in April 1865. Thomas fought throughout the Atlanta campaign, seeing action at Dalton, Resaca, Kennesaw Mountain, Peachtree Creek, and the Battle of Bald Hill (Atlanta). Following the war, Thomas served as chief of police of the city of Atlanta and as sheriff of Fulton County.

Following the Battle of Bald Hill (Atlanta), Federal troops such as these pictured here occupied their own trench lines around the city while the Confederate army settled in for a long siege: "We are still standing quite [quiet] since our big fight on last Friday," wrote Evan Park Howell of Howell's Battery, Georgia Light Artillery. "We occupy the ditches around town, and the enemy just in front of us; sharp shooting and cannonading now and then. The enemy shell the city once in a while, doing no other damage than kill a few women and children."

An attorney from Monticello, Georgia, James Stoddard Boynton served in the Vicksburg campaign and from Chickamauga through the Atlanta campaign until wounded at the Battle of Bald Hill (Atlanta). Six months later, he returned to duty on crutches, commanding his regiment until its disbanding. In 1883, Boynton succeeded Alexander H. Stephens as Georgia's governor. (Note: the blackened right eye is the result of an imperfection in the original ambrotype portrait.)

Members of the Bomar family, who lived on the Marietta road, were located close to the city fortifications and underwent severe shelling during the siege. Homes and businesses in northwest Atlanta were particularly hard hit. Newspaper reports in November noted all the homes on Marietta Street had been damaged by artillery.

Stationed in the lines around the city, Confederate forces did more than wait out the siege—they fought back. "Where we lay now," wrote Sergeant William Jack of Connecticut, "we can see two Reb forts quite plain on a hill directly opposite us and yesterday and this morning they have been amuseing themselves by throwing shell at us, we can see the puff of smoke come out of their works and down goes our heads...."

Next to burned-out ruins of the Atlanta Lard Oil Factory, the Macon & Western rail line begins its great bend as it turns south from a northwesterly route out of Atlanta. The curved building at right center is the Macon & Western Railroad locomotive house on Hunter Street (Martin Luther King Jr. Drive).

City treasurer John Henry Mecaslin, in the uniform of Fire Company No. 1, served in the 3rd Battalion of the Georgia State Guards during the siege. In early 1864, Mecaslin, a grocer, became chief of the volunteer fire department, which worked to control fires from the bombardment.

Mayor Calhoun's son, William Lowndes Calhoun, here with wife Mary Jane Oliver, worked as a partner in his father's law firm. During the war, he was captain of the Calhoun Guards No. 2, Company K, 42nd Georgia Regiment, until he was detached and commanded the military post and prison at Madison, Georgia. Fighting in the retreat from Dalton, he was severely wounded at the Battle of Resaca, May 1864. Following the war, he served as mayor of Atlanta in 1878.

A conductor for the Atlanta & West Point Railroad, James Lorenzo Bell served in the Davis Infantry, Company K, 7th Georgia Regiment, from 1861 until surrendering at Appomattox Court House in 1865. Reportedly, he single-handedly captured an entire Federal regiment, the 19th Wisconsin, during an engagement near Fair Oaks, Virginia, in late 1864. For years, a commendation for this act, signed by Robert E. Lee, hung in his home.

"That red day in August..." August 9, 1864, was the worst day of the siege. Solomon Luckie, a free African American, ran a barber shop and bathing salon in the Atlanta Hotel. While at the corner of Whitehall and Alabama Streets that day, Luckie was struck by shell fragments from the bombardment. Taken by Thomas Cruselle (p. 24) and others to the Atlanta Medical College, Dr. Pierre-Paul Noel D'Alvigny (p. 126) amputated his leg. Suffering from shock, Luckie failed to recover and died a few hours later.

Luckie and his wife, Nancy Cunningham, were two of the less than 40 free African Americans living in Atlanta in 1860.

In 1854, shoemaker Christian Kontz built this home on Marietta Street, near the current site of the Federal Reserve Bank. Kontz also maintained a homestead along present-day Fourteenth Street. During the siege of Atlanta, Kontz's house was within range of Sherman's artillery. Following the war, the house was the official residence of Generals Pope, Meade, and Ruger, successive military commanders of the Southeast during Reconstruction.

In late July, General Hood's headquarters were located in a tent behind the L. Windsor Smith residence on Whitehall Street. Isabella Gray Ryan lived on Whitehall and remembered the street as "a thoroughfare for the soldiers, and through its dusty opening the dead and dying were borne." Ryan recalled "young men in the flush of health and beauty and old men determined, and blanched, pass my gate . . . leaving a bloody trail in the dust as they tottered by."

Planter and slave trader Ephraim G. Ponder moved to Atlanta in 1857, when he built a grand home on a high knoll north of the city. Constructed of white-plastered stone and surrounded by terraced gardens, boxwood, and fruit trees, the house was topped by an observation deck, providing a splendid view from its hill-top prominence. In 1861, however, Atlanta society was shocked by scandal; filing for divorce, Ponder charged his wife, Ellen Gregory, with adultery among various men, continual drunkenness, abusive language, disrespect, and threatening him with a pistol. Though the divorce was not final until 1871, Ponder moved to Thomasville, Georgia, leaving the estate in the hands of his wife, who refuged to Macon during the war. Ironically, the vantage point that influenced the Ponders to build their house on the site also motivated Confederate engineers to construct defense works along the approach to the house. The house served as a perfect sharpshooter's position for Southern forces and subsequently a perfect target for Federal artillery in the woods near present-day Eighth Street. Reportedly, a ton of shell and shot was found within its walls.

After moving to Atlanta around 1848, William Richard Venable worked as bookkeeper to the Forsyth cotton merchants (p. 26). In 1856, he was elected clerk of the superior court, acting as custodian of the city records. Venable, his wife, Cornelia Hoyt, and family lived on the city's northwest side on Marietta Street near Foundry Alley and the Western & Atlantic rail line. When the shelling of Atlanta began, their home was in a particularly hazardous location. "I was here during the war," she recalled, "I remained through the siege, and not until Sherman's army entered the city did I leave." The Venable family sought shelter in a pit dug in their garden, like the one shown on the opposite page; with room only for the children to lie down, Cornelia and her mother slept sitting up. The Venables and three children were among those still in Atlanta when ordered out by Sherman, leaving with 25 packages of clothes and other possessions. Tradition maintains Venable also left with Atlanta's records for safekeeping.

Those who could, built bombproof structures or "pits" in hills or in gardens to escape the artillery. Lucy Caldwell used the pit in her neighbor's yard, which was dug six feet in the ground and covered with timber and earth. "Within was laid a carpet and a few chairs," she recalled, "thither we would go, when the shelling began." Even the embankment of the secluded Walton Springs, once the fashionable promenade spot for the city residents, became home to caves in the hillside. Yet even those in the pits would never forget the whizzing zip and the terror of the bursting shells. "How I wish the federals would quit shelling us and we could get out of the cellar and get some fresh air," Carrie Barry wrote in her diary. "The shells get worse and worse every day."

Pictured here are Martha Powell (p. 28) and her children, Frank and Ella May. The Powells remained in the city until July, when they sought refuge in Newton County. "My husband and I took our children in our arms," she recalled, "and left the house as General Sherman's army began shelling the town. I shall never forget that night of terror as we were escaping."

Son of Luther J. Glenn (p. 38), Howell Cobb Glenn's namesake was his maternal uncle, Howell Cobb, who served as U.S. congressman, governor, secretary of the treasury under President James Buchanan, and as president of the provisional Confederate Congress prior to the election of Jefferson Davis.

Pictured here are the children of Dr. and Mrs. Benjamin F. Bomar (p. 34–5), Amaryllis and Thomas Haynes Bomar. Shortly after the fall of Atlanta, Thomas wrote to his sister about "our old home." "The vile invader," he expressed, "has polluted with his vandal hordes that soil which has been hallowed to us by the happy hours of childhood."

Looking from Fort Hood, *chevaux-de-frise* protect a cannon redoubt overlooking the Ponder House on the northern perimeter of Atlanta's defenses. A palisade runs beyond the main house and its stripped-bare outbuildings, which provided the lumber for the fortifications. Not far

from this commanding hill, Mayor Calhoun surrendered the city on September 2. Fort Hood was the northwest corner of an extended Siege Line constructed in late July in response to Sherman's field guns, located only a short distance away.

Attorney James Montgomery Calhoun served as wartime mayor for four terms, 1862–66. On the morning of Friday, September 2, Calhoun surrendered the city at a location beyond Fort Hood near present-day Marietta Street and Northside Drive. Opening the city to Federal troops, Calhoun affirmed: "The fortune of war has placed Atlanta in your hands," and asked for the protection of citizens and private property. Sherman, however, issued an order evicting civilians from the city. Mayor Calhoun instructed residents: "You must all leave Atlanta . . . ."

Jane Louisa Killian Crew, the wife of James R. Crew, a ticket agent for the four rail lines serving Atlanta, is shown here. The Crews remained in Atlanta throughout the siege. When Sherman proposed a ten-day truce to permit the evacuation of residents, one of the men chosen to deliver the offer to General Hood was James Crew. In 1881, the widowed Mrs. Crew became the second wife of Lemuel P. Grant (p. 45).

On the night of September 1, the Confederate cavalry destroyed what they could not take with them: the munitions not transferred while the rails were still open. This *Harper's Weekly* illustration portrays the resulting explosive destruction of Hood's ordnance train. "The R.R. cars and engines," wrote S. P. Richards, " were all run up to one place in order to be fired just as the enemy left." The resulting blast of five locomotives, 81 rail cars, and siege guns, shells, and other materiel devastated the nearby Confederate Rolling Mill and burned into the early morning hours. "As we went down the Ammunition Train was fired," Richards continued, "and for half an hour or more an incessant discharge was kept up that jarred the ground and broke the glass in the windows around. It was terrific to listen to . . . ."

The ruins of the Atlanta Rolling Mill are pictured here, following the destruction of Hood's ordnance train. Founded in 1858, the rolling mill produced railroad iron and later manufactured cannon, iron rails, and plating for naval ironclads. Situated along the Georgia

rail line southeast of downtown, the rolling mill site is now home to parts of Oakland Cemetery and the former Fulton Bag and Cotton Mill.

With the entrance of Federal troops into Atlanta, residents were guaranteed their property would be respected by the occupying soldiers. "I was therefore very much surprised," S. P. Richards wrote, "when I went down to see armsful and baskets full of books and wall-paper going up the street in a continuous stream from our store and when I reached the store, the scene would have required the pencil of Hogarth to portray."

Four

YANKEES IN ATLANTA

On September 4, 1864, Sherman turned Atlanta into a military encampment. By virtue of Special Order No. 67, he expelled the residents of the city. Following weeks of bombardment and starvation, the families of Atlanta were forced to abandon their homes. Arguing against the command, Mayor Calhoun wrote to Sherman hoping to overturn the order and the ensuing hardships: "You know the woe, the horror, and the suffering cannot be described by words." Sherman's response: "War is cruelty, and you cannot refine it . . . ."

Some residents traveled to homes of relatives throughout Georgia and the South, but many others had nowhere to go. Residents were permitted to carry a limited amount of property with them, but with transportation problems brought about by war, even that could only be done with great difficulty. By agreement with Sherman, household furniture was gathered together and placed for safekeeping in Trinity Methodist Church, located on Mitchell Street opposite city hall. But most of this was lost in the looting and destruction surrounding the Federal army's movement out of the city. A great deal of personal property was simply abandoned by residents at the time of their exile.

In all, nearly 2,000 residents left, carrying almost 9,000 packages of clothes, personal property, and household belongings. Using wagons supplied by the Federal army, residents transferred as much as they could collect to the Car Shed for loading onto box cars. From there, Atlantans traveled to the Rough & Ready depot in Clayton County, where they were transferred to Lovejoy Station to board trains heading south. George B. Cadwallader, of the U.S. quartermaster's office, reported "On the 10th I took charge of all transportation for the delivery of the citizens of Atlanta and their Baggage to the Confederate authorities at Rough & Ready, a station on the Macon and Western Rail Road 12 miles from the city. This work was executed in ten days and required the use of 100 teams and 30 Ambulances each day."

William G. Forsyth (p. 26), who hoped to remain in Atlanta, finally headed north with his family and a few friends on the eve of the destruction of the city. His daughter, Annie, recalled two cattle cars were provided and, upon arriving in Nashville, Tennessee, they found themselves "homeless, penniless, and half-starved," camping on the roadside in tents. While there, they lived in a damp, infested factory basement, where they suffered from dysentery and lost a daughter to the illness. The Forsyths, like many Atlantans, later returned to the devastated city and their burned-out homes.

Bookseller S. P. Richards, who kept a diary, served in Company H, 3rd Battalion, of the Georgia State Guards. He lived with his wife, Sarah Van Valkenburgh, on Washington Street and ran a business with his brother, Jabez. Expecting the arrival of Federal troops, Richards stated: "Sallie and I have about decided to stay at home, Yankees or no Yankees. We hear and read terrible tales of them, but I don't think they are as bad as they are said to be."

A Federal supply convoy proceeds up Peachtree Street past the Georgia Railroad & Banking Company Agency building and turns left onto Marietta Street at what is now Five Points. The bank, chartered by the city of Augusta in 1833, was constructed in 1856 and was destroyed when Sherman evacuated Atlanta for the March to the Sea. The photograph of the destroyed building is one of Barnard's most celebrated images (p. 124–5).

With the possessions of refugees piled high on the top of boxcars, Atlanta residents wait at the Car Shed for one of the trains to leave Atlanta for Rough & Ready. "We were ordered out . . ." lamented Cornelia Venable, "and the citizens had to go find homes wherever they could."

Assembling on Wadley [Forsyth] Street at the office of Lieutenant Colonel C. F. Morse, Federal provost marshal, residents register to obtain passes to leave Atlanta. Morse allowed refugees to carry food, clothes, and a limited amount of furniture.

A contemporary woodcut depicts furniture and other possessions being loaded into U.S. military wagons. Sherman's eviction order stated: "The city of Atlanta being exclusively required for warlike purposes, will be at once vacated by all except the armies of the United States . . . ."

Cotton factor and merchant Robert Flournoy Maddox and his wife, Nancy J. Reynolds, pose for a whole-plate ambrotype in the Whitehall Street studio of William H. DeShong in 1861. Moving to Atlanta in 1858, Maddox organized and served with the Calhoun Guards No. 2, 42nd Georgia Regiment, fighting at Vicksburg and Missionary Ridge. After the war, Maddox was president of the Maddox-Rucker banking firm and the Old Dominion Guano Company.

A Federal wagon train sits on Alabama Street looking east from the corner of Whitehall Street toward the Georgia Railroad locomotive house. This area is now the heart of Underground Atlanta. The white building at right is the Atlanta National Bank and next to it, the Franklin Printing House & Bookbindery.

Sitting on wheelbarrows and caissons and standing with shovels and picks, a Federal construction crew takes a break during completion of Fort No. 12, located in southwest Atlanta in the area of present-day Phoenix Park.

The firing step, allowing troops to step down into the trench to reload, runs along the bottom of the line in a view of Federal Fort No. 13, located where the Atlanta-Fulton County Stadium once stood.

After occupying Atlanta, the Federal army constructed fortifications concentrated within the existing Confederate works. Following in this chapter is a series of photographs displaying the new Federal line. Sherman and his staff are shown at Federal Fort No. 7; seated fourth from left in civilian clothes is Chief Engineer Orlando M. Poe, responsible for the new line of defense.

Troops pose in Federal Fort No. 7, previously Confederate Fort D, incorporated into the new defense. The western-most redoubt of the Federal line, it stood on high ground located in the heart of the current Clark Atlanta University campus.

A visual icon of the Atlanta campaign, this is one of Barnard's most famous images of the city. The Crawford, Frazer & Co. slave market was located at No. 8 Whitehall Street between Alabama and Hunter [Martin Luther King Jr. Drive] Streets. L. C. Butler remembered the benches surrounding the room on which slaves were seated. "Here," he said, "the prospective buyers made their selections just as they would have a horse or mule at a stockyard."

The 111th Pennsylvania Volunteers fill Atlanta's original Public Square, running between Pryor and Loyd Streets, next to the rail line. Along with State Square on the south side of the depot, this property was auctioned in November 1870 for commercial development. Just beyond Decatur Street is Masonic Hall (right) and the Trout House, constructed by Jeremiah Trout in 1854. This was the city's largest hotel and served as the reception site for President Jefferson Davis's visit in 1861. When Trout left the city with his wife, Amelia, and five children, they carried a whopping 60 packages of personal goods.

Edward E. Rawson had four daughters; Mary, Carrie, Laura, and Eunice. During much of September 1864, Mary kept a diary recording the battles and subsequent evacuation of Atlanta.

Rawson and his wife, Elizabeth Clarke (below), moved to Atlanta in 1857 and established Rawson, Gilbert & Burr, a hardware business. Two years later, Rawson built The Terraces (above), a prestigious residence encompassing an entire city block along Pryor Street on the south side of Atlanta, where some of the most fashionable homes were located. A city councilman from the second ward, Rawson served in Ezzard's Company of the Georgia Infantry during the war. The Terraces acted as Brigadier General John W. Geary's headquarters during the occupation.

This is another view of Federal Fort No. 7, looking southeast toward Fort No. 8, situated west of present Walnut Street.

Federal Fort No. 10 overlooked the Macon & Western Railroad, which connected with the Atlanta & West Point Railroad at East Point. In late July, this was the only rail line still open to Atlanta.

Constructed with *facine* (bound bundles of sticks) to reinforce the earthworks, this view of Fort No. 20 looks across the Georgia Railroad, running through the center of the image. By mid-July, Sherman had dismantled this rail line east of Atlanta.

Positioned astride the rail line south of current Decatur Avenue, Fort No. 20 guards the eastern approach to Atlanta. The scene looks northwest across tracks of the Georgia Railroad. The cupola of the Atlanta Medical College rises just beyond the tree at left.

Shown here are Emma Mims Thompson (left) and her husband, Dr. Joseph Thompson (below). Mrs. Thompson was known for her singing in local programs, her voice being "of the finest quality." She later served as president of the Board of Women Managers of the 1895 Cotton States and International Exposition. A South Carolina native, Dr. Thompson practiced medicine in Decatur for a number of years. Shortly after completion of the rail line into Marthasville, he became proprietor of the Atlanta Hotel (opposite), situated at the corner of the railroad and Pryor Street, and served as president of the Atlanta Medical College.

Federal troops sit atop boxcars on the rail line next to the Atlanta Hotel. In the distance rises the pediment of the Masonic Temple. The roof line at right, just above the locomotive, is the Macon & Western Railroad's Rock Depot built by Thomas Cruselle (p. 24).

Atlanta's manufacturing output expanded during the war, often incorporating production facilities from Nashville, New Orleans, Memphis, and other captured cities. Thanks to the city's extensive rail lines, which came together in the city's principal rail yard (above), Atlanta also became the center of a fabrication network, uniting manufacturers from Selma, Columbus, Macon, Augusta, and other Southern industrial cities.

With sewn timbers and graded earth, Fort No. 9, east of the current University Park, exhibits nearly perfect emplacements indicating the time, material, and manpower available to the Federal army compared to the Confederate fortifications.

The wheelbarrows on which the men sit and the gun and timber at right, still waiting to be placed, show that Fort No. 11 was nearing completion. The white building in the center background is the L. Windsor Smith residence, which served as General Hood's headquarters.

Looking north on Washington Street, the home of Georgia State Supreme Court Judge Richard F. Lyon stands at the corner of Mitchell Street, opposite city hall. Built in 1859 by John Neal, the Lyon residence served as Sherman's headquarters. Following the war, Lyon was forced to sell the house at auction, where it was reacquired by John Neal. Never used as a residence again, it later served at various times as Oglethorpe College, Boys' High, and Girls' High. The building was torn down in 1928 for the current city hall.

Jared I. Whitaker served as Atlanta's initial wartime mayor until he resigned in November 1861 to accept appointment as Georgia's commissary-general.

The *Atlanta Daily Intelligencer* newspaper office, located above Wittgenstein's saloon, stands at Whitehall Street and the railroad tracks. Founded as the *Madison* [Ga.] *Southern Miscellany* in 1842, the *Intelligencer* was the only newspaper to survive the war. Published by Judge Jared I. Whitaker (opposite below), the newspaper lost many of its readers and advertisers because of its Reconstruction views, forcing it to close in 1871.

Guarded by a sentry and showing evidence of defense works surrounding city hall in the right foreground, the William Solomon residence on Mitchell Street served as the Federal army's post headquarters during the occupation of Atlanta, September–November 1864.

Two Federal soldiers pose on the impressive columned piazza of the Austin Leyden residence on Peachtree Street. Completed just before the war, the house was built by John Boutell Jr. (p. 30) for merchant William Herring, but was also occupied by the family of Leyden, his son-in-law. This house served as General George H. Thomas's headquarters during the occupation.

The chimney remains of buildings at the end of Alabama Street stand with the Western & Atlantic Railroad freight warehouse in the background. "After the war was over," wrote Cornelia Venable, "we returned home to find our house in ruins and the city a heap of ashes and debris."

Five
DESTRUCTION

Sherman spent two months in Atlanta. When he departed he left the ruins of the city in his wake. Sherman ordered the destruction of all buildings and material that could later be of use to the Confederacy; what could not be consumed or loaded in wagons was burned, torn down, blown up, or disabled in some manner. "Colonel Poe had been busy in his special task of destruction . . . ," Sherman wrote, and had "leveled the great depot, roundhouse, and the machine shops . . . . The heart of the city was in flames all night . . . ."

Lucy Pittman recalled Federal troops placing straw and other flammable substances into stores and houses to be burned "in order to destroy the entire city." When buildings were too large or heavy to set afire, such as the Car Shed, they were blown up or destroyed with battering rams. To add to the scene, the Atlanta gas works was torched, sending flames shooting into the sky. "The town," Pittman said, "looked like the infernal regions."

When destruction efforts were complete, everything of a railroad, industrial, or military nature was gone: train depots, warehouses, foundries, mills, and armory. Any type of machinery not consumed by fire was rendered useless. A government report later noted: "nothing has escaped." Whitehall Street in particular faced heavy losses. As the primary commercial district, nearly half of the city's merchant businesses were located here. "All business houses and many dwellings were burned," wrote Mary Luckie, "I remember standing on Whitehall Street, near Mitchell, and looking around to see only ruins, chimneys, and charred walls north, south, east, and west." In addition to the commercial loss, an estimated 3,200 residences were destroyed, as well as the surrounding forests—"for miles around scarcely a tree is standing."

Terminating his communication and supply lines from the north, on the morning of November 16 Sherman and his staff rode out of the city via Decatur Street en route to Savannah. Within days of Sherman's departure, residents began the task of rebuilding the city, and later chose the ancient phoenix rising from its ashes as Atlanta's symbol.

Two soldiers stand next to bonfires used to heat railroad track, illustrating the use of the tool used to twist softened rails. Twisting the track guaranteed Confederates would not be able to simply bow them back again for reuse. The Western & Atlantic Railroad Freight Warehouse appears in the background.

With the ruins of the Car Shed at right, soldiers demonstrate methods used to pull entire sections of track to loosen spikes attaching rails and ties. Ties were then used as bonfire fuel over which rails were laid, softening them to bend and twist into "Sherman's neckties." The men became skilled at the practice, with teams performing each step in the process.

Smoke from bonfires fills the air as Federal troops prepare to destroy a boiler and other materials.

A detail from *Harper's Weekly* illustrates the devastating fires in Atlanta as Federal troops marched out of the city.

As the Western & Atlantic Railroad roundhouse burns, Federal soldiers continue their destructive work in the foreground.

A detail from a *Harper's Weekly* shows the ruins of the Georgia Railroad roundhouse as the city burns. (The cupola of Fire Engine House No. 2, at left in this illustration, also appears at far left on p. 120–1.)

The remains of the Car Shed appear at center in a contemporary illustration of the ruins in Atlanta.

Much of the devastation in the central city is cleared and rebuilding is underway in this 1866 image. In the foreground, engines from the Atlanta & West Point and Georgia rail lines sit on the turntable amid the rubble of the Georgia Railroad locomotive house on McDonough Street

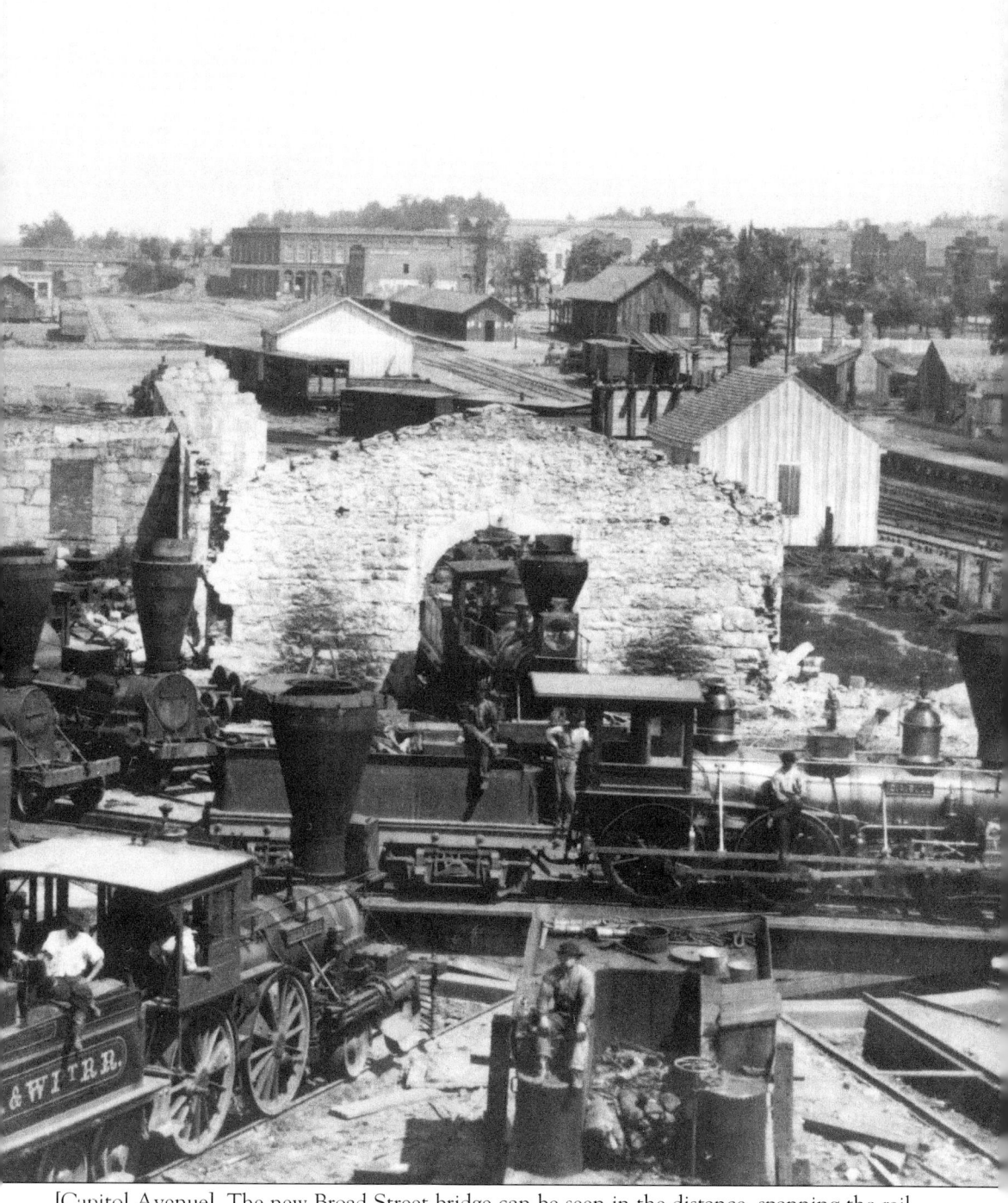

[Capitol Avenue]. The new Broad Street bridge can be seen in the distance, spanning the rail lines.

Images such as this one of the engine house and machine shops of the Western & Atlantic Railroad in September 1864 (above) contrasted sharply with scenes documenting the destruction of Atlanta's rail lines and railroad facilities, such as the Car Shed (opposite). While the city quickly rebuilt its basic transportation framework, it was not until 1871 that a suitable rail station was constructed to appease city leaders. At that time, the new Union Passenger Depot replaced a makeshift wooden structure on the Car Shed site.

Often erroneously identified as an example of the vagaries of war, this scene of Brown & Dwyer's billiards and saloon hall adjacent to ruins of the Georgia Railroad bank does not indicate a Yankee love of game and liquor. This Barnard photograph was taken roughly two

years after the war, by which time a saloon had been built on the remains of a previous structure.

Paris native and French army veteran Dr. Pierre-Paul Noel D'Alvigny received a medical degree from Indiana University and assisted on the Atlanta Medical College's faculty. Serving as a Confederate hospital, the medical building (below) was slated for destruction by Federal troops. Tricking Federal officers, D'Alvigny filled the clinic's evacuated beds with hospital attendants pretending to be wounded patients. Surprised, the officers gave D'Alvigny until daylight to clear the building—by then, however, the March to the Sea had begun, and the college was saved.

Born in Charleston, South Carolina, Sarah Moses married Aaron Alexander, moving to Atlanta in 1848 when her husband established a drug business. Sarah founded the first Jewish Sabbath School. At that time, the couple also built a residence on the east side of Peachtree Street. Leaving Atlanta in 1859, they settled in Columbus, Georgia, where they remained for the duration of the war. Opposed to secession, the Alexanders' sons nevertheless served in the Confederate army. When reported of her son Julius's bravery in battle, Sarah Alexander replied: "Pity it was not done in a better cause." Like other wartime refugees and exiles, the Alexanders returned to Atlanta in 1865. They then moved into their previous home and founded a successful hardware business.

Acknowledgments

Above all, I would like to thank two people: William Fulmer Hull, Atlanta History Center staff photographer, for without his excellent reproductions this book would not exist; and Arif Khan, for his detailed research and layout assistance, and for being there at both the beginning and at the end, in each case when it counted most. Also, thanks go to Kimberly S. Blass, the Center's editorial director, for her support and wise admonitions; Gordon Jones and Myers Brown, the Center's military historians, for their lessons and corrections; Anne Salter, director of the Atlanta History Center Archives, for her support; and Franklin M. Garrett, for his incomparable *Atlanta and Environs*, an incredible wealth of fact and detail.

Michael Rose
Visual Arts Archivist
Atlanta History Center

Resources

Atlanta: A Portrait of the Civil War showcases the wealth of images in the Atlanta History Center's visual arts collection, from beautiful daguerreotypes and other cased images to a number of rarely reproduced Civil War photographs. For further readings and photographs on the Atlanta campaign, see:

Ambrose, Andy, and Darlene R. Roth. *Metropolitan Frontiers: A Short History of Atlanta.* Atlanta: Longstreet Press, 1996.

Carter, Samuel III. *The Siege of Atlanta, 1864.* New York: St. Martin's Press, 1973.

Castel, Albert. *Decision in the West: The Atlanta Campaign of 1864.* Lawrence: University Press of Kansas, 1992.

Davis, Keith F. *George N. Barnard: Photographer of Sherman's Campaign.* Kansas City, Mo.: Hallmark Cards, Inc., 1990.

Garrett, Franklin M. *Atlanta and Environs: A Chronicle of Its People and Events.* Athens: University of Georgia Press, 1954.

Garrett, Franklin M. *Yesterday's Atlanta.* Miami: E.A. Seemann Publishing, Inc., 1977.

Hoeling, A. A. *Last Train from Atlanta.* New York: Thomas Yoseloff, 1958.

McCarley, J. Britt. *The Atlanta Campaign: A Civil War Driving Tour of Atlanta-Area Battlefields.* Atlanta: Cherokee Publishing Company, 1989.

Scaife, William R. *The Campaign for Atlanta.* Atlanta: William R. Scaife, 1985.

Voices of the Civil War: Atlanta. Alexandria, Va.: Time-Life Books, 1996.